CONTENTS KU-498-830

2019001209

INTRODUCTION

ACKNOWLEDGEMENTS

Paul and Alan would sincerely like to thank their wives – Susan and Kerry – for their help and support during the writing of this book. In particular Kerry for knocking up spectacular salads (with warm potatoes!) to keep us going, providing endless refreshments, and Susan for her thorough checks and honest feedback on the content.

We would also like to thank Julia Philpott for writing the breakdown in the communicating strategy scene setter. Also, Andy Cross for inspiration and for the team dynamics scene setter.

Disclaimer

To the best of our knowledge, these icebreakers are original. If we have inadvertently picked up similar ideas from looking at other publications, please accept our apologies as this was never intended.

THE
ICEBREAKERS POCKETBOOK

By Paul Tizzard & Alan Evans

Drawings by Phil Hailstone

"Paul and Alan are two of the best trainers I have worked with; they have a talent for opening people's minds to learning. I'm delighted that they have been able to share some of their ideas and passion in this book – a great stimulus for any trainer."
Andy Cross, Head of Training, UnumProvident Limited

"These icebreakers are refreshingly new and stimulating for all types of event, from opening a meeting to running a large conference...a facilitator's dream book!"
Marina Haughian, Learning & Development Consultant, City & Guilds

"I have worked with Paul Tizzard on a variety of training programmes he has designed and delivered for Virgin Atlantic Airways. He has never failed to surprise me in his use of new and creative ways of engaging people in learning events. This book will be a source of inspiration!"
Vanessa White, Learning & Development Consultant, Virgin Atlantic Airways

Published by:
Management Pocketbooks Ltd
Laurel House, Station Approach, Alresford
Hampshire SO24 9JH, UK
Tel: +44 (0)1962 735573
Fax: +44 (0)1962 733637
E-mail: sales@pocketbook.co.uk
Website: www.pocketbook.co.uk

This edition published 2003. (Reprinted 2004, 2005)

© Paul Tizzard & Alan Evans 2003

British Library Cataloguing-in-Publication Data – A catalogue record for this book is available from the British Library.

ISBN 1 903776 05 8

Design, typesetting and graphics by **Efex Ltd**   Printed in UK

PURPOSE OF THIS POCKETBOOK

The aim of this book is to give anyone involved in training others some memorable ways of opening their workshops. We feel strongly that there is a place for **tailored** icebreakers and scene setters. Trainers are often busy without much time to research and develop new ways of giving their training more impact. Also, looking for suitable icebreakers for particular workshops is time-consuming. We have saved you time by categorising the scene setters into common course themes for your easy reference.

In this book, you will find 40 tailored activities that work best when used to introduce a session on a particular topic. We would recommend that you use a fairly standard form of introduction before moving on to any of the activities, such as the 'paired interview' style of introduction. We have separated these activities into different categories, which are shown on the contents page.

How to use the activities

We suggest you have a read through and then do the TMS test. In other words, That Makes Sense test. When you see some activities that you like, experiment with them, distort them and adapt them to the groups that you work with.

FOREWORD BY JOHN TOWNSEND

Congratulations to Paul and Alan for putting together this **FABULOUS** collection of icebreakers!

These 40 activities are **F**ast-moving, **A**musing, **B**ridged/linked to course content, **U**nique, **L**ively, **O**ptimistic, **U**ncomplicated and in most cases **S**hort (5-10 minutes). I like the longer ones (15-30 minutes) too because they all involve the learning of models and theories at the same time as being fun and challenging.

A big plus for me is that each icebreaker is explained clearly and succinctly with full details of objectives, materials needed, process to follow and even possible variations trainers can use.

All in all a great addition to the Pocketbooks range of hands-on help for trainers. Forty fabulous icebreakers – fabulous value for money!

John Townsend
Master Trainer Institute

ASSERTIVENESS

GET INTO SHAPE

Aim
A fun way to start an assertiveness course

Learning
Demonstrate how they deal with uncomfortable situations

Materials
One bendy person per delegate (These are sold in places like www.thetrainingshop.co.uk)

Trainer knowledge needed
An understanding of the four behaviours of assertiveness, namely passive, aggressive, assertive and passive-aggressive. Refer to *The Assertiveness Pocketbook* for further reading

Process

1. Ask the group to pick up the 'bendy person'

2. Say something like, 'when I am faced with an uncomfortable situation, this is what I feel and look like…'

3. Ask them to mould the bendy person into what represents how they feel

4. Go round the group one by one and ask them to tell everyone else (Option 1)

5. Ask them to form groups of four to five people and tell the individuals in that group only (Option 2)

6. Ask them to shape the person to how they would like to look when dealing with situations (Option 3)

What's the point?

Assertiveness courses often touch on areas that people prefer to leave unsaid.
The course will be of a very superficial nature if these areas are not ever mentioned.
The idea of this activity is to get the information about how people feel in that situation without just asking them outright. This is also a very good leveller, as it will let everyone know that they all feel the same or similar.

WHAT WOULD YOU DO?

Group size
Minimum of
3 - maximum
of 15

Time
15 minutes

Aim
To introduce some of the core concepts of assertiveness in a light-hearted manner

Learning
Discuss the theory of passive and aggressive behaviour

Materials
Prompt cards made out with the following scenarios:

1. 'You and your partner walk into a restaurant and you are directed to a table near everyone else. One area of the restaurant appears to be kept deliberately clear by the waiting staff. You would rather sit there, away from other people and nearer the window. You suggest this to the waiter, who looks a little annoyed. What would you do?'

2. 'You have been in a new job for about four weeks when your boss walks in and says to you, "milk and two sugars please". What would you do?'

3. 'You are waiting in an airport security queue and it is moving very slowly. You are concerned about catching your flight and starting to feel a bit agitated. You notice that someone has pushed in your queue about three places in front of you. You hear a couple of people "tutting", "sighing" and making sarcastic comments. What do you do?'

Trainer knowledge needed

An understanding of the four behaviours of assertiveness – passive, aggressive, assertive and passive-aggressive plus an understanding of the behaviour iceberg model.

Like an iceberg our visible behaviour represents the tip, and is on display for all to see. Below the surface lurks the unseen part of the iceberg, which represents the bigger part of ourselves – who we actually are – our feelings, beliefs, culture, etc.

The behaviour iceberg asks, 'are you displaying behaviours which are consistent with the message you are trying to get across, or are unhelpful feelings creeping up into your behaviour and distorting the message?'

Process

1. At the beginning of assertiveness course, split the group into three

2. Give out a card to each group and ask them to consider what they would do in response to what it says

3. Review their thoughts as a large group

4. Link to later modules around the course content. Scenario one relates to what you believe your rights are. Scenario two relates to what you think you are obliged to do when you work for someone else. Scenario three introduces the concept of passive-aggressive behaviour and not confronting situations assertively

What's the point?

Situations to be assertive in are all around us. It is important to identify situations which you should assert yourself in and those in which you shouldn't.

Variation

Split the groups and ask them to write scenarios for the other groups to think about. Structure the thinking around the following areas: What would you do? How would you classify the behaviours? What options do you have when dealing with situations?

PHOTO GALLERY

Group size
Any

Time
25 minutes

Aim
Highlight the differences between assertive and non-assertive behaviours

Learning
Relate your ideas about assertive and non-assertive behaviours to famous people

Materials
Laminated photos of famous people
On large paper or four sheets of flip paper taped together, draw a huge red triangle with the words Assertive, Passive and Aggressive written at each corner

Trainer knowledge needed
Difference between assertive and non-assertive behaviour

Process

1. Introduce the subject of assertiveness. Cover and clarify the difference between assertive and non-assertive behaviours
2. Ask your delegates to choose three from a variety of laminated photos of famous people (leaders, film stars/characters, etc)
3. Ask the delegates to list three behaviours they have witnessed in each of the people in their pictures, which fall under the label of assertive, passive or aggressive
4. Based on behaviours they believe the characters display most, ask the delegates to plot the photos on the large assertive, aggressive, passive triangle
5. Facilitate the link between how they drew their conclusions and the way others draw conclusions about us
6. Ask group to plot own names on triangle, based on where they think others see them
7. Conclude: we all move between assertive, aggressive and passive continuously and for different reasons. If you have learned to spend *some* time being assertive, you can learn to spend *more* time being assertive. This is our goal

What's the point?

Assertiveness is a learned skill and as such requires practice.

Variation

Use photos of non-famous people who have personalities only you are familiar with. Let group make their conclusions, based on appearance. Share truth with them at end!

SERGEANT SILLY

Group size
12 maximum

Time
30 minutes

Aim
Evoke an assertive attitude through dressing to be assertive

Learning
Demonstrate the effect of appearance upon our ability to be assertive

Materials
Prizes (eg: sweets)
Military hat, stick, jacket, boots (all x 3)
Ridiculous attire, eg: wigs, clown's feet, squirty flowers, etc (x 3)

Materials cont'd
Cards, that read:

'Your task is as follows:
Demonstrate how assertive behaviour typically looks
and sounds.

In order to do so you must communicate three
statements. The topic is up to you. You decide upon,
plan, and write out the content of your three statements
in terms of types of words to use, tone, pitch, speed and
volume, and body language to adopt.

One of you must don the attire to make your statement.
The other must be prepared to explain the thinking behind
the content.

You have ten minutes to prepare to communicate your
three statements to the group. Points will be
awarded, based on the above criteria.'

TO BE
OR NOT
TO BE

Trainer knowledge needed
General knowledge of assertiveness. For further reading, see *The Assertiveness Pocketbook* by Max Eggert

Process
1. Introduce assertiveness and prepare the group to take part in an activity
2. Delegates pair up. Give all pairs a task card. Refer them to the laid-out attire to choose from – they may not mix 'n' match, but must take either a complete set of military or a complete set of ridiculous attire. Ask if there are any questions
3. After the ten minutes expires, request that each pair deliver their statements in the attire provided and adhering to their agreed criteria. Maintain an upbeat pace and atmosphere

Note: Some pairs will be wearing military attire, others the ridiculous attire

4. Discuss the activity in a large group. Did the way they looked affect their performance?

Process cont'd

5. Award ten points to each pair per assertive behaviour identified.
   Give bonus points to anyone delivering assertive behaviour while dressed
   ridiculously, as this is more difficult to do. Award prizes

6. Make the connection between looking assertive and feeling assertive by asking
   questions, eg: did the clothing affect your ability to deliver each statement? In what
   way? What are the psychological implications?

7. Refer to the pre-written statements by each pair. What was the thinking behind these?
   Do you think they were assertive statements on reflection? What would you change?

What's the point?

We often assume the role we believe people expect of us.
Looking assertive can help us to feel assertive.

COACHING & MENTORING

SPOT THE COACH

Group
size
Any

Time
20 minutes

Aim
To get some grasp of what coaching is about

Learning
Define what coaching is

Materials
Enough copies of the suggested scenario cards (shown over page) for
each person
Flipchart

Trainer knowledge needed
Clear understanding of what coaching is and isn't. Suggested reading:
The Tao of Coaching by Max Landsberg and *The Coaching Pocketbook* by
Ian Fleming

Process

1. Give out the cards to your group (four people per group)

2. Ask them to consider:
   - Which of these scenarios is coaching and which is not
   - Be prepared to explain your reasoning

3. After ten minutes, review the answers as one large group. You need to pull out the bits that relate to coaching (see over)

What's the point?

By using everyday conversations, you will help people to see what is coaching and what it definitely is not.

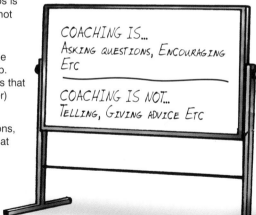

COACHING IS...
ASKING QUESTIONS, ENCOURAGING ETC

COACHING IS NOT...
TELLING, GIVING ADVICE ETC

Scenario A

Gary: How did you think that meeting went?

Chris: It was okay - I suppose

Gary: You don't seem sure

Chris: I think that I could have handled the disruptive people better

Gary: In what way?

Chris: Well, maybe if I had been a little firmer with people

Gary: What could you have done?

Scenario B

Raj: I can't stand that Marina girl

Rachel: If I were you, I'd go for lunch with her and sort it out

Raj: I've tried that but it doesn't work

Rachel: How about confronting her then?

Raj: That doesn't work either

Rachel: Perhaps you should change jobs

Raj: um

Scenario C

Vanessa: I've got a really angry customer on the phone and I don't know what to do

Terri: What do you think you should do?

Vanessa: They want money back and I don't know what my authority is or what I should do

Terri: Okay, well do what you think

Vanessa: Er, thanks. 'Hello Mr Smith...'

Scenario D

Team leader speaking to her team.

Emma: I need some help with preparing the budget for next year. Is there anyone who can help me?

Suli: I would be very happy to help you if you give me some guidance

Emma: Of course. We will go through it together and you can take on as much as you feel comfortable to do

Some suggested answers to scenarios:

Scenario A
This is coaching. Use of open questions to draw out the person's thinking. Picking up on the subtlety of what was said. Some probing questions used.

Scenario B
This is not coaching. Giving advice is helpful, but not coaching.

Scenario D
This is demonstrating the use of responsibility as one of the coaching principles. Suli will now be committed to helping as he volunteered. Had Emma just picked someone, they may not have taken the same amount of responsibility for the task.

Scenario C
This is not strictly coaching. It is about recognising that sometimes you should just tell people the answer. The coaching comes in, after the phone call, to review what happened and decide what worked and what didn't.

Link
The scenarios could be linked to the TA icebreaker *TA Quips!*, see page 51

COACHING & MENTORING

GROW YOUR PEOPLE

Group size
Minimum 4 -
no maximum

Time
20 minutes

Aim
Make the principles behind coaching memorable

Learning
Identify the boundaries of a coach's role
Use the standard skills of a gardener to understand the principles behind coaching

Materials
Several cards, each one containing one of the following words: 'Seed', 'Earth', 'Water', 'Pot' and 'Sunshine'
One pack of seeds/bulbs and flowerpots for everyone
Plus: earth, water, newspaper, flipchart and small card

Trainer knowledge needed
An understanding of the fundamentals of coaching. Awareness of the GROW model desirable, but not essential (see *Coaching for Performance* by John Whitmore)

Process

1. Introduce the topic of coaching, giving particular emphasis to how individuals are responsible for their own development. The manager's role is to enable the person to grow by providing the right conditions, etc

2. Allow everyone to pick a seed of his or her choice. Discuss the merit of picking what seems to be the right one for them. Link to staff recruitment on how you choose what seems like the best candidate at the time

3. Ask everyone to plant the seed in one of the provided pots of earth, and water it

4. Split the group into smaller groups and give them a different card each

5. Give them five minutes to think, 'how are each of the different things I have just done symbolic of a manager's role?'. Examples might be: a 'seed' is like the member of staff – has potential but needs nurturing; 'water' is a regular thing a seed needs to grow, like feedback and one-to-ones

6. After five minutes, discuss in a large group and plot on flipchart. Reiterate that coaching is about the manager providing the tools for growth – they can't **make** anything or anyone grow, only enable

What's the point?
All answers are correct. However, you are hoping that they will discuss how a manager can only **enable** a member of staff to grow. The manager's job is to provide the necessary conditions for individuals to grow but, ultimately, they could remain dormant for no apparent reason.

COACH

20

COACHING SKILL/WILL

Group size
Enough to form four teams of equal numbers (ideally 12 people)

Time
20 minutes

Aim
To provide a solid experience of the skill/will model

Learning
Experience different types of motivation levels

Materials
Pre-prepared flipchart drawing of skill/will model
Lots of coins of varying sizes
Briefing cards (see later)

Trainer knowledge needed
Good familiarity with the skill/will model and thorough grasp of coaching.
For further reference see *Coaching for Performance* by John Whitmore and
Leadership and the One Minute Manager by Ken Blanchard

Process

1. Split group into four equal teams and give them a table each. Each table should be given one briefing card per team

2. Briefing cards should have the following instructions:

   A. Your task is just to sit there and do nothing

   B. Your task is to balance your ten coins on top of each other on their sides. It will take a lot of skill to do this – you may not be able to achieve it

   C. Your task is to make as many patterns as possible in five minutes with your ten coins. You can have as much fun as you like. This is no trick – just enjoy playing with them. If your patterns are better than the other teams', you may get a prize!

   D. Your task is to walk around and observe the other teams and give them whatever support, positive feedback or guidance you see fit, in your experience. The tutors trust you to do what is right

3. Give them ten minutes to complete their task

4. Ask for feedback on how they felt during the exercise. Probe to find out how they felt at the beginning of the exercise, compared to how they felt by the end of it

What's the point?

The point is to bring out the feelings associated with each of the four squares in the model.

- Brief card A represents low will and low skill. That team should feel quite flat at the end of the exercise

- Brief card B requires high skill. Also, as the task is very difficult, it will not be very motivating to do – hence low will

- Brief card C represents low skill and high will, because it is quite motivating but requires very little skill

- Brief card D represents high will and high skill, as you are totally trusting the individuals to do what they feel is right

COACHING - SAY WHAT?

Group size
Any

Time
30 minutes

Aim
For people to experience the different stages of the GROW coaching model

Learning
Identify and discuss the GROW model

Materials
Four boxes or folders
Card for backing
Pictures of light bulbs, footballs and people running
The GROW questions separated into 'goals', 'reality', 'options' and 'will', laminated and cut out into separate questions
Copy of newspaper for the day of the course

Trainer knowledge needed
Familiarity with John Whitmore's coaching model is essential as is a thorough understanding of coaching principles. A full list of the questions for each stage are provided in John Whitmore's book *Coaching for Performance*. Some examples are listed below:

Goals
What are you trying to achieve?
How much influence do you have over your goal?
What would you gain/lose if you were to attain your goal?

Reality
What is happening now?
What are the barriers?
What have you tried already?

Options
What could you do?
What are you going to do?
How will you overcome barriers?

What/Will
What are you going to do?
When are you going to do it?
What support do you need?

Process

1. Stick each 'goal' question to its own backing card, along with a cut out picture of a football

2. Do the same for all other questions, pairing up the 'reality' questions with the newspaper cuttings, the 'options' questions with the pictures of light bulbs and the 'will' questions with the pictures of running people

3. Put all 'goal' questions in a box; do same with 'reality', 'options', and 'will' questions

4. Split the group into smaller groups and give them the four boxes

5. Ask them to open the boxes in order of the GROW model and to lay the sheets out in whatever order they feel would be appropriate

6. Allow them 30 minutes to look over the questions and get used to how they work in each of the separate sections

7. Review the session by simply asking, 'at a first glance, how do they strike you?' Some answers will comment on how open the questions are, and how non-judgemental they are. There are no right or wrong answers to this

What's the point?

This will familiarise delegates with the questions that make up the GROW model. It is more likely to be memorable if they have a chance to 'discover' patterns themselves.

COACHING & MENTORING

MENTORING

Aim
Form an effective mentor/mentored relationship

Learning
Identify the difference between coaching
and mentoring
List the criteria of a typical and effective
mentoring relationship

Materials
One large plant in a pot
Handful of other potted plants of varying sizes
A couple of plant seeds or bulbs

Trainer knowledge needed
You will need to be familiar with the subtle difference
between coaching and mentoring. Refer to *Everyone
needs a mentor* by David Clutterbuck

**Group
size**
Any

Time
20 minutes

Process

1. Before delegates arrive on your mentoring course, place the plants
   and seeds on a table in the following order, clearly visible at the front of the group:

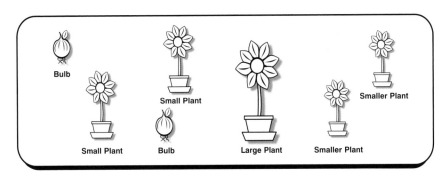

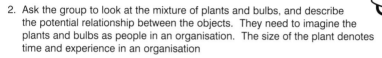

2. Ask the group to look at the mixture of plants and bulbs, and describe
   the potential relationship between the objects. They need to imagine the
   plants and bulbs as people in an organisation. The size of the plant denotes
   time and experience in an organisation

3. Ensure you have a mixture of bulb and plant types on display, and make this obvious.
   Delegates may then draw the links to important factors to look for when choosing a
   mentor, eg: a bulb should choose, as a mentor, the plant it **aspires to be**. No point in
   a cheeseplant looking to be inspired by a daffodil!

4. Position some of the bulbs and plants close to each other, and some far apart.
   This is representative of links in reporting lines and raises the question, 'should my
   mentor be close to me, eg: be my manager or my manager's manager, or can he or
   she work elsewhere?'

5. Ask them to consider, in small groups, which combinations would make the best
   mentoring relationship. Another question to prompt their thinking: 'which couplings
   would make for an ideal coaching relationship?'

6. Collect the comments onto a central flipchart

7. Link the answers to what will be covered during the course

What's the point?
The point is to bring out the difference between the two approaches.
Mentoring relationships tend to be between a very experienced person and someone who is 'up and coming' in an organisation, such as a graduate or someone on a fast-track programme. Coaching can involve anyone, although it tends to be between manager and employee.

In plant terms, the large central plant would be considered the typical mentor and perhaps paired up with a smaller plant. Plants of a similar size would not usually be mentors but could coach each other. Large plants and bulbs/small plants that are too close to each other may mean that the larger plant has something to gain or lose by the speed and quality of the bulb's/small plant's development. This is inappropriate – ideally, there should be some distance.

COMMUNICATION

COMMUNICATION

FIRST IMPRESSIONS & ASSUMPTIONS

Group size
Any

Time
10 minutes

Aim
Convince people of the importance of first impressions

Learning
Discuss how first impressions are formed based on behaviour only

Materials
None

Trainer knowledge needed
An understanding of the iceberg model and of how your behaviour forms people's first impressions. (The iceberg model is described on page 5). Trainer needs to be quite brave with this icebreaker

It only works with people who do not know one another very well

Process

1. At the beginning of the course, ask everyone to pick a partner whom they do not know

2. Ask them to write down their comments relating to the areas below, without showing them to their partner:

   - Where their partner grew up
   - What sort of car they drive
   - Where they live
   - What their hobbies are
   - What sort of person they are
   - What they do to relax

   The aim is to guess the answers, based on what they can see

3. Give them five minutes to write their answers down. Ask them to put their partner's name on the front of a piece of paper and then hand it to you for safe-keeping

4. Tell them that they will get their forms back later when you introduce the importance of first impressions and how they are formed

5. Introduce the concept of the iceberg model or something similar before they start the exercise

(33)

What's the point?

The point is that people form an impression of you from what you say and what you do. There are two parts to this: you need to be aware of how you come across; you can put on a persona to create a strong first impression even if you are nervous.

Variation

1. Use on Assertiveness courses to highlight how you can make people believe you are assertive even if you don't feel it

2. Ask the whole group to observe you at the beginning of the course and answer the same questions about you. If they do it in groups, it is a good talking point for them and it shows you as very open and brave. This is particularly good if you intend to ask them to role-play later on in the course as it shows you are not above being given feedback. This is also a fantastic opportunity to show how to receive constructive and positive feedback

Link

Can also be used on Assertiveness, Facilitation and Train the Trainer courses.

BUSINESS WRITING

**Group
size**
Any

Time
10 minutes

Aim
Cause delegates to keep written communication simple and to the point

Learning
Simplify a written notice
Laugh at overcomplicated, pompous notices

Materials
A copy of this notice (found in a public toilet) for each delegate:

'It is anticipated that at times, this convenience may not be to the required standard of cleanliness. Should this occasion arise, do not hesitate to tell the management, so that they may give the matter their fullest attention.'

Trainer knowledge needed
An understanding of how to write a concise message (examples
from Campaign for Plain English – www.plainenglish.co.uk)

Process

1. Give everyone a copy of the notice
2. Allow them ten minutes in pairs to rewrite the notice to make it clearer
3. Review the ideas by discussing what they have come up with
4. Accept all contributions as valid and then link to what you will be covering in the course

What's the point?

Dispel the myth of a need for long pompous messages and promote a need for written communications to be kept simple.

Variation

1. Instead of discussing their contribution, ask them to rewrite it in large letters on a flipchart (more risky for them though)
2. Ask them to bring some of the literature from their own building to analyse (again, there is a higher element of risk here and more chance of offending the host organisation)

COMMUNICATION

NEGOTIATION SKILLS

Group size
Any

Time
15 minutes

Aim
Use everyday examples to get people thinking about how they could negotiate more

Learning
Identify everyday scenarios where negotiation skills would be an advantage

Materials
Copies of brief cards

Trainer knowledge needed
A good understanding of negotiation skills is essential

Process
1. Split group into mini groups of around 4-5 people
2. Give out the brief cards to each group
3. Ask for their comments and then link to remainder of course

Example brief cards:

Scenario A
You are desperate to buy a car and have a budget of £2,000. You see something you like in a local showroom for £2,400. When the sales person approaches, you offer £2,200 but the sales person says that they most definitely cannot take anything lower than the asking price. You really want the car but it is a little above what you would like to pay. What would you do?

Scenario B
You walk into an expensive jewellers to buy an engagement ring. You see something you like and you buy it at the stated price. A couple of weeks later, you bump into a friend of yours who has also shopped at the jewellers. Your friend tells you quite proudly how she managed to get 25% off the price of a ring she bought at the same shop. What could you or would you have done differently?

Scenario C
A double glazing salesperson is talking to you in your home. He offers you four windows for £4,000 and then (without you asking) gives you a 50% discount if you were to buy today. You decline. Minutes later, your home phone rings and it is the salesperson's alleged boss who offers you another 20% off the already discounted price. The boss is putting quite a lot of pressure on you to buy the product today. You really want some windows. What are your thoughts of the product now and what would you do?

Scenario D
You are about to meet a supplier to negotiate a new business contract. What do you need to know to be able to prepare yourself? What questions do you need to ask yourself?

What's the point?

Examples of negotiating are out there all the time. The point is to raise delegates' awareness of when they could use more negotiation skills. Some pointers:

Scenario A

This is linked to two things. The first is having in your mind what would be your highest, middle and lowest offers. The second part is knowing if you are willing to walk away from something that you wanted

Scenario B

People rarely negotiate in places like jewellers, as this can appear 'cheap and tacky'. The truth is that there will be quite a high mark-up on their products for that very reason

Scenario C

Be aware of the 'tricks of the trade'. Ask your friends to find out what they have had pitched to them lately. What techniques are they aware of?

Scenario D

The importance of preparation

Variation

Ask delegates to come up with examples, in small groups, of one time when they negotiated well and felt pleased with themselves, and another time when they felt that it didn't go well at all. Take examples of each per group.

PASS THE PARCEL

Aim
To get the point across behind 'probing questions' in a fun way by playing 'pass the parcel'

Learning
Practise using probing questions

Materials
Music and stereo
Pre-wrapped parcel (many layers) with 'freebies' inside

Trainer knowledge needed
A knowledge of probing questions and their uses is essential here.
A good source would be Terry Gillen's book *Positive Influencing Skills*

Process
1. Pre-wrap a parcel in as many layers as there are people on your course

2. Inside the parcel put some sweets or prizes for them to win

3. Every time the music stops, whoever has the parcel has to ask the trainer a probing question. After the first person has asked their question and you have answered it, the next person that gets the parcel has to ask a question that is probing, open and follows on from the last question

4. Keep going until all the layers have been opened and the freebies found

What's the point?

This will get your delegates trying out probing questions in a fun and lighthearted manner. There are no wrong answers, only learning.

Variation

Insist that their questions fulfil the criteria for probing questions and that they don't get to unwrap anything until they get it right. Between each piece of wrapping paper, put something linked to the course material. The 'prize' inside the parcel could be directly linked to the course. For instance, on one of our courses we put Boost bars inside for the delegates. Boost was also an acronym for feedback: Balanced Observed Owned Specific Timely.

Link: This could also be used for Coaching courses.

COMMUNICATION

WE'RE GETTING THERE!

Group size
Any

Time
10 minutes

Aim
Encourage delegates to transmit messages with the recipient in mind

Learning
Discuss the concept of 'congruence' in communication
Identify the benefits of communicating messages while placing the importance on style of delivery

Materials
Tape player
Pre-recorded announcement from train station during delay. (The idea for this one came while one of the authors was waiting for a train that then became delayed. To explain the delay, a pre-recorded message came over the public address system that had parts of the sentence almost 'cut and pasted' in. The message was like the one below, with the italic text denoting the parts 'dropped in'.)
'Ladies and gentlemen, we are sorry that the train to *Sutton* is going to be *delayed* by *twenty* minutes. We are sorry about the inconvenience that this may cause you.'

Trainer knowledge needed

An understanding of the importance of the message you want to give sounding genuine

Process

1. Play the tape recording to the whole group
2. Split the group into smaller groups of three
3. Ask each group to consider for five minutes how they felt upon hearing the message. Did it sound genuine? Why? What would be the impact on you if you were in a hurry?
4. Discuss the different groups' thoughts on the matter
5. Introduce the concept of how the content of messages you send, which are backed up by other sub-messages you send during delivery, are the ones which **will** achieve the desired aim
6. Ask for any other humorous examples the group may have of messages not backed up by the way they were delivered

What's the point?

To take a light-hearted look at communication gone wrong – albeit with good intention.

Variation

If it is difficult to record a copy of a delay message, you could read it out using a nasal voice and a bit of drama.

(43)

WHERE'VE YOU BEEN?

Group size
Minimum 6 -
no maximum

Time
5 minutes

Aim
Cause thinking about the need for clear communication

Learning
Discuss the experience of being on the end of a poorly communicated message

Materials
Post-its in the shape of arrows and/or cards with words or pictures to be used as signposts

Trainer knowledge needed
No content knowledge. However, you will need to know how to facilitate the learning point from a potentially annoyed group of people!

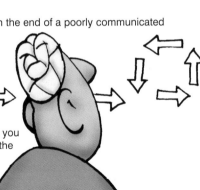

Process

1. Badly sign the route to the training room or coffee area with your Post-it arrows/cards

2. When delegates eventually find the place, ask them at some point after the initial introductions, 'how does it feel to be on the end of a poorly communicated message?'

What's the point?

Relate this to any form of communication that people send out without thinking it through. The impact of the miscommunication can destroy all the good intention behind it.

Variation

1. Badly sign a route or room that the delegates are familiar with. You could use this to highlight the power of what Janis called 'group think'. Ask, 'why did you follow the instructions as given?' If they didn't fall for it, ask 'why not?' and 'what did you think differently from those who did just blindly follow the communication?'

2. Sign the route too well. This means putting so many signs up it becomes annoying or humorous. This brings out the concept of telling people too much sometimes

3. Give the route out in written form, prior to the course on writing skills. Make the instructions either over-wordy or minimal. Again, this is to emphasise communication in the written format

COMMUNICATION

WHAT I MEANT WAS ...

Group size
Minimum 4 - maximum 14

Time
20 minutes

Aim
Convey your idea accurately

Learning
Discuss factors affecting your ability to communicate an idea effectively

Materials
Flipchart and pens

Trainer knowledge needed
Communication skills

Process
1. On a flipchart facing the wall, out of the sight of delegates, write:
   - Enjoy the benefits of using good communication
   - Discuss the problems that can occur when communicating
   - Learn a lot about each other's communication styles, and have fun too

2. Ask for a volunteer to help you with an experiment
3. Overtly, brief the volunteer that they must:
   - Try to convey the messages in their own unique way
   - Avoid reading aloud what is on the flipchart
   - Do so in no more than two minutes
4. Tell the group: 'there are three parts of an idea written down that our volunteer will try to convey to you. Your job is to write a summary of what you believe the message to be'
5. Give the volunteer two minutes to convey the messages
6. Ask each group member for their interpretation of the messages
7. Reveal the original messages
8. Discuss the volunteer's behaviour used, including body language, tones and words used to convey the messages. Ask the volunteer what they were thinking when using these methods, and the audience what they were thinking when observing these specific behaviours
9. Make the link to the way we receive incoming information, based on what it means to us once we have 'filtered' it

What's the point?
It is easier to discuss effective/ineffective communication based on our experiences. This is one way of providing everyone with an experience they can relate to and discuss their interpretations of.

TELL 'EM WHAT YOU'RE GONNA TELL 'EM

Group size
Minimum 4 -
maximum 12

Time
10 minutes

Aim
To persuade people to add 'signposting' to their communication
skills arsenal

Learning
Practise using a signposting technique
Appreciate the importance of letting people know what you are thinking
before launching into a different view from theirs

Materials
Two - four toy 'walkie-talkies'

Trainer knowledge needed
You will need a grasp of the signposting theory of communication.
In other words, the ability to signal what you are about to say before
you say it

Process

1. Split the group into two or four subgroups (depending on how many walkie-talkies you have)

2. Give out the walkie-talkies to each group. (You will have already preset the channels to different frequencies without telling the group)

3. Ask them to interview each other about the weekend or favourite hobbies

4. When they can't get through to each other, lead the review about why it could be. Ask how it felt not being on the same wavelength as someone else. Ask them what they need to do to be able to communicate with someone else

What's the point?

When people communicate with each other, they frequently assume that the other person sees the situation in the same way. It is all too common to experience discord during meetings and one-to-one discussions due to misunderstanding about where the other person is 'coming from'. This exercise is designed to simulate what it is like to try and communicate with someone not on the same channel or wavelength as you.

Variation

1. Use walkie-talkies on a telephone skills course and ask them to tell each other about their weekend or something quite detailed, and try to remember what was said. Ask them to think about how much of the message they missed. What are the 'rules of etiquette' around the use of mobile phones? What are the limitations of the phone versus face-to-face contact? What are the advantages of the phone over face-to-face contact?

TA QUIPS! (TRANSACTIONAL ANALYSIS)

Group size
Any

Time
20 minutes

Aim
Use quotations to work out what 'game' someone is playing in transactional analysis (TA) terms

Learning
Identify the key giveaway signals when someone is playing a 'game'

Materials
Scenario cards for every group

Trainer knowledge needed
Keen knowledge of (TA). A good book is *TA Today*. It is also worth visiting www.adinternational.com run by established TA expert Julie Hay

Process
1. Give out the scenario cards to groups
2. Ask them to look at the cards and decide what sort of 'game' is being played; suggest they look for clues in the words being used
3. Review the feedback
4. Link to rest of course and what you will be covering

Scenario A
Raj: *It's not fair. Everything seems to go wrong for me. It's not fair*

Scenario B
Raj: *I can't seem to get this report right, no matter what I do*
Vanessa: *Maybe you need to walk away and come back to it later?*
Raj: *I've done that but it didn't help*
Vanessa: *Can I help you with it?*
Raj: *You could, but I guess you won't understand it*
Vanessa: *Anyone else can help?*
Raj: *Not really, no one really understands what I do or has time*

Scenario C
At bus stop
Clare: *I can't believe how long it takes for a bus these days*
Sue: *I know. Nowadays, no one really cares about us old folk waiting in the cold*
Clare: *That's right. And when they do turn up, it is some kid driving who doesn't care*
Sue: *Absolutely, just the other day...*

What's the point?
People play games all the time and this helps to identify the clues that give it away.

TA & REALITY

Group size
Any

Time
10 minutes

Aim
Introduce transactional analysis

Learning
Use the theory of parent-adult-child
in transactional analysis

Materials
Tape player/microphone
Pens and paper
You will need to spend
some time recording
people speaking about
everyday things such as the
weather, buses being late, etc

Trainer knowledge needed
Good understanding of TA

GOO GOO GAR GAR

Process
1. Play the recording of the voices at the beginning of a session on transactional analysis
2. Ask them to shout out what type of voices they can hear. Do they sound 'childlike' or 'parent-like' or 'adult-like'?
3. Use their comments to link into the ego states of TA

What's the point?
If you have recorded good examples of each state – eg: the neutral tone of voice of the adult; the caring voice of the nurturing parent; the harshness of the critical parent; and the excitement or over-politeness of the child – they will have a very clear introduction to what the ego states are about.

Variation
1. Record people in your office and ask them to give you rehearsed recordings for your voices
2. Give your group enough recorders to do their own version. Tell them that they have to come up with voices saying the words for each state in the theory. They need to come up with the answers unprompted by you – you can correct later when you go through the theory

CUSTOMER SERVICE

WEALTHY CUSTOMER

Group size
Any

Time
20 - 30 minutes

Aim
To expose customers as being sources of wealth

Learning
Use a new perspective of the customer to serve them with fresh insight

Materials
Pens and paper

Chart with:

4 letters 5 points	1-5 words 100 points
5 letters 10 points	5-10 words 200 points
6 letters 20 points	10-15 words 300 points
7 letters 30 points	15-20 words 400 points
8 letters 50 points	20+ words 500 points

Trainer knowledge needed
None (but see *The Customer Service Pocketbook* for further reading)

Process

1. Split your group into pairs and write 'CUSTOMER' on a flipchart
2. Ask each pair to come up with as many words as they can from the letters in the word 'CUSTOMER' in five minutes
3. Before beginning, ask each pair to write down a guess as to how many words they expect to identify in the time allocated, the number of letters in their longest word and the points they believe they will earn
4. Add up scores at the end
5. Ask how their predictions compare with their results
6. Ask how their performance expectation compares with the expectation others had for themselves
7. Did you exceed or fall short of your expectations? Why?
8. Cheesily make the link from the exercise carried out to the fact that our CUSTOMERS are a rich source of wealth. Ask how we can make sure we mine them for more wealth. What can we do that we are not already doing?

What's the point?

This is really just a bit of fun to kick-start your customer service course, but it also makes the tongue-in-cheek point that customers are often not paid attention to, after an initial attack of good quality service.

Variation: Use any other word relevant to your session.

(57)

CUSTOMER SERVICE

THIS IS A LISTENING SKILLS ONE, DAVE

Group size
Any

Time
5 minutes

Aim
For delegates to realise how important small details are when listening to someone else

Learning
Discuss the importance of getting a person's name correct when listening

Materials
Flipchart
Pens

Trainer knowledge needed
Minimal

Process

1. Introduce 'listening' as being a basic part of good customer service

2. Draw two columns on a flipchart with 'Names' at the head of one column and 'Variation' at the head of another

3. Write the names of your delegates in the 'Names' column

4. Ask group for the most humorous, annoying or ridiculous variation of their name, which they have been called at any point in their lives

HEE HEE WINKLEBOTTOM HA HA HA HA

5. Write the names they come up with in the 'Variation' column, against their actual names

6. Light-heartedly and briefly discuss the impact these variations had on them, and the feelings they evoked. Draw the links to the impact of poor listening in a customer service situation

7. Pin the flip-charted names/variations on the wall for the remainder of the course. Hark back to them occasionally as you see fit

What's the point?
Customers who are judging your service on the interpersonal skills you display will not feel listened to if you do not get even minor details correct.

PEOPLE MANAGEMENT

PEOPLE MANAGEMENT

NEW TEAM LEADER

Group
size
Any

Time
20 minutes

Aim
To get new team leaders sharing their common experiences of being
a new supervisor or team leader

Learning
Discuss new team leader situations

Materials
Copies of brief cards for every group

Trainer knowledge needed
Minimal knowledge. Suggested reading: *The Starting in Management
Pocketbook* by Patrick Forsyth

Process
1. Put group into smaller groups of four to five
2. Give out briefing cards
3. Review their answers as a large group

Example cards:

Scenario A
You have been recently promoted from within your own team. Some of your previous work colleagues now report to you

3/5 don't like it. They have started to make comments under their breath when you ask them to do anything. You know that they are talking about you during their lunch breaks

What would you do?

Scenario B
You have been recently promoted and your boss has suggested to you that you shouldn't go to lunch with your ex-peers as they now work for you and you are management

Do you agree with this?

What would you do?

What's the point?
This gets people talking about common situations that can occur when
they have been promoted. The point is to help them realise that people
feel the same way about the situation.

Variation
Split the group into equal teams. Ask them to come up with the worst situation
imaginable that has or could happen to a new supervisor/team leader. They write it up
and then you collect the answers. Redistribute the scenarios to the other groups to
discuss and solve.

PEOPLE MANAGEMENT

MANAGER AS DEVELOPER

Group size
Any

Time
15 minutes

Aim
To help managers use a model for debriefing staff, who have learnt something new, either about themselves or on a course

Learning
Identify questions to ask their staff after a learning or development opportunity has occurred

Materials
Brief cards written out for each group

Trainer knowledge needed
Sound knowledge of Kolb's learning cycle and probing questions

Process
1. Introduce the concept of Kolb's learning cycle and how people learn. Explain that people need to go through all four stages of having an experience, reflecting upon it, concluding and planning what to do next
2. Split group into smaller groups and give out one brief card per group
3. Review the thoughts and questions the groups come up with
4. Link back to the learning cycle

Suggestions for debrief:

Brief 1 – examples
How was the course?
What were the highlights?
What did you learn?
What will you put into practice?

Brief 2 – examples
How did you feel the meeting went?
How do you think the other participants thought it went?
What would you do differently next time?

Brief 3 - examples
What in hindsight would you do differently?
What was different from the last time you ran it?
What were you pleased with?

Brief 4 – examples
What did I contribute to the way it went?
What would I do next time it happens?
What could I have applied that I have learnt before?

Brief 1
Using the model of Kolb's learning cycle, consider how you would use great questions to review a member of staff who has returned from an offsite training course. What questions might you ask to bring out the learning?

Brief 2
You have just witnessed a member of your team run a meeting that did not go too well. After the meeting, you decide to speak to her. What might you ask, using Kolb's learning cycle, to bring out the learning?

Brief 3
A colleague of yours has recently come back from running an induction training session. He is not very happy with his performance

Using Kolb's learning cycle, what might you ask to bring out the learning?

Brief 4
You have just received a phone call from an angry customer. You don't feel that you dealt too well with it

What questions might you ask yourself to take yourself through the learning cycle?

What's the point?
The point is that the learning cycle has been around for a long time and is held up to be very valid. This exercise gives people applied ways of stepping into it. Of course, there are many other ways that it can be used, but this is just a start.

PEOPLE MANAGEMENT

COMMUNICATING STRATEGY

Group size
3 - 15

Time
15 minutes

Aim
Persuade middle to senior managers of the importance of putting passion behind words, when setting a vision or goal for their departments

Learning
Discuss the importance of emotive vision/goal setting
Discuss what and how feelings are evoked in us by others

Materials
Stereo
Piece of music (please see example on page 70 or use your own)

Trainer knowledge needed
Basic strategic awareness. Otherwise limited, if you use the provided example

Process

1. Split group into groups of three or four

2. Play piece of music and ask them to listen to it

3. Talk them through how the music was put together. Give them a technical breakdown of its musical components

4. Then, ask how the music makes them feel. Ask, 'what was the story behind it?' 'What is the composer inviting us to feel?'

What's the point?

The point of the exercise is that people can feel the passion behind something without needing to know the technical background to it. In terms of setting goals or vision for people, don't get caught up making them measurable and technically correct, if it doesn't mean anything to the receiving audience.

WE ALL LIVE IN A YELLOW SUBMARINE

Variation

Use a piece of famous poetry instead of music.

Example of music for this exercise:

> **Gustav Holst's 'Mars' (from the 'Planets Suite')**
>
> **Key technical points for the facilitator to highlight:**
>
> - This piece is written with 5 beats to a bar - this is quite unusual (we are normally used to hearing music with 2, 3, 4 or 6 beats in a bar). Listen for the emphasised beat and you will be able to count up to 5 before the next emphasised beat
> - The composer has different instruments playing in different keys that clash against one another (D flat minor and C minor). This is what creates the uncomfortable, discordant sound to the music
> - The stringed instruments (violins, violas, cellos and double basses) are told to play 'col legno' which means they use the wooden part of the bow to strike the strings. Again, this is an unusual technique used deliberately to produce a rattling sound
> - In a similar way, the timpani (kettle drums) are instructed to use the hard end of the stick (rather than the soft 'pom-pom' end)

Overall effect created:

- The planet Mars was named after the Roman god Mars - The Bringer of War, which is the full title that Holst gave to this piece. By bringing together all of these different technical effects Holst conjures up an image of a threatening army marching to bring destruction and devastation to whatever it meets in its path

- The slightly more hopeful tone to the middle of the piece suggests that there may have been defending troops that believed they had a chance against their attackers, but they are soon crushed by the power and momentum of the invading army

- The piece ends with a series of dramatic concluding 'blows' and an air of finality that suggests that this Bringer of War would take no prisoners

Narrative: Julia Philpott, UBEVCO

Note: Please check your company's music licence

CHANGE MANAGEMENT

Group size
Maximum 15

Time
15 minutes

Aim
A very visual way of demonstrating the dynamics of teams when problem-solving

Learning
Discuss a model of team dynamics when problem-solving

Materials
Four 'runner bean' type canes
Lots of varied objects such as: Koosh balls, stress balls, rolled up flipchart paper and any other obscure objects

Trainer knowledge needed
A thorough understanding of problem-solving processes and what can happen. A knowledge of the 'storming' model could also be helpful

Process

1. Set up the objects similar to the diagram on page 75 (Stage one)

2. Ask people to stand outside the canes

3. Say, 'when you put people together for a brainstorming or problem-solving session, this is what will happen to them, to a greater or lesser degree...'

4. Then give the objects a big shove with your foot. The objects will now spread themselves into clusters and separate objects (Stage two)

5. Ask, 'if these are your people, what is happening to the different groups? What is happening with the people (objects) that are ahead of the others? For the people (objects) that are still stuck together, what is going on there?'

6. There are no right or wrong answers

7. You could ask them to explain what the facilitator has to do to move the people on from where they are

What's the point?
The point is to make it memorable for when they are next facilitating a problem-solving session. The exercise is visual and involves them standing up and looking over the model.

Variation
Ask them to stand in the model and to walk through it, describing the likely stages and emotions as they go through it. Other people not acting as the 'pawns' could say how they would help each person through the different stages.

Source: Andy Cross, UnumProvident

Example of what model could look like:

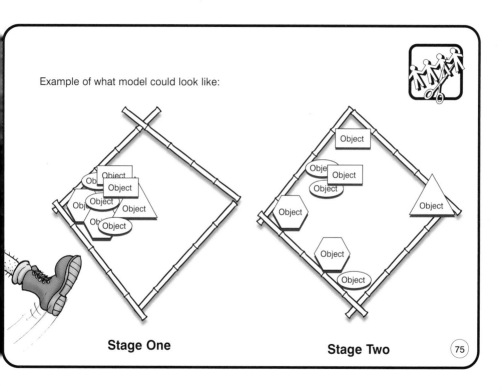

Stage One

Stage Two

PEOPLE MANAGEMENT

MANAGEMENT STYLES

Group size
Any

Time
15 minutes

Aim
For people to work out their management style, using short quotes from the leadership continuum

Learning
Identify statements that link to four styles of leadership

Materials
Cards with statements written on (enough sets for group size – one set per four people)
Flipchart

Trainer knowledge needed
You need to be familiar with Tannenbaum and Schmidt's model of leadership. The Tannenbaum and Schmidt leadership continuum can be found in Pfeiffer's theories and models

Process

1. Draw the leadership model (see below) on a large piece of paper
2. Give out the statement cards and ask the people, in groups of four, to identify where the statements belong on the continuum
3. Ask them to think about where they prefer to be and perhaps do the same for people who they have worked with
4. Ask them which style is suitable for which situation

Examples of statement cards and flipchart drawing:

A. "Leave it with me."	
B. "Do what you like."	
C. "Please go ahead and then check with me."	
D. "Here's a problem – tell me what you think and then I will make a decision."	

What's the point?
To make this excellent model very accessible to anyone at any level.
Suggested answers:

A = Manager takes all responsibility (directive style – left hand side)

B = Manager takes little responsibility (totally empowered style – right hand side)

C = Manager asks to be involved in decision-making (semi-empowered)

D = Manager involves her staff (democratic)

Variation
1. Use the method above, but change the cards to personalise to your company. You could make the comments much harder to identify. If you would like to add more to the model, you can add as many cards as you wish to emphasise the subtlety

2. Draw a huge version on the floor. Ask people to move up and down it. As they go through each stage, ask them to demonstrate that type of leader; what they might look like and what they might say

PEOPLE MANAGEMENT

MOTIVATION - MASLOW

Group size
Any

Time
20 minutes

Aim
Encourage managers to address the needs of their staff in an order of priority based on Maslow's hierarchy of needs

Learning
Identify the different layers of Maslow's hierarchy of needs model
Discuss what they can do as managers to address each level

Materials
Enough shoe boxes for each level of the hierarchy model
Marker pens to write each level's name on the boxes
Cards (small enough to fit inside the boxes)
Large inflatable hammer (not essential)

Trainer knowledge needed
Thorough understanding of Maslow's model
Refer also to *The Tao of Motivation* by Max Landsberg and *The Motivation Pocketbook* by Max Eggert

Process
1. Introduce the hierarchy of needs model
2. Show them your pre-prepared model. This will have all the shoe boxes stacked on top of each other. On the side of each one will be the name of the level, eg: Safety, Esteem, etc (inside each box place a card on which you have written the major components of that level, eg: Safety = safe environment, security in the situation, etc)
3. With great theatrical effect, announce that you cannot get to the 'Self-actualisation' level at the top, unless you have satisfied the needs at the lower levels. Pause for a moment, then swing your hammer at the bottom box causing the rest to come crashing down
4. Emphasise verbally again what has just occurred, ie: that without the bottom box, or need, in place, the rest won't exist either
5. Now ask the group to divide into sensible groupings and to pick up one box per group. Ask them to open the boxes and to read the cards inside
6. Ask them to adapt the theory to what a manager needs to do at a practical level to satisfy that need. Then review the whole group's ideas

What's the point?
To help them understand in a visual and quite dramatic way that they need to work with all levels for a person to reach their potential.

Link: This links in neatly to coaching, as coaching is the best way to develop people once they are in the top two layers of Maslow's hierarchy.

PEOPLE MANAGEMENT

MOTIVATION - HERTZBERG

Group size
Any

Time
10 minutes

Aim
Teach managers what preparations must be complete before they can hope to be effective in motivating their staff

Learning
Recognise the importance of the hygiene factors being met when trying to motivate others
Link the building of a house to Hertzberg's model of motivators and hygiene factors

Materials
One doll's house or equivalent
Four shoe boxes to act as 'stilts for the doll's house'

Trainer knowledge needed
Full knowledge of Hertzberg's theory
Refer also to *The Tao of Motivation* by Max Landsberg

Process

1. Prepare four shoe boxes by writing on all of their sides one hygiene factor per box, eg: 'pay' on one, 'pension scheme' on another. You will need to have picked four of what you would call the most critical of the hygiene factors

2. Stand them up so that they can support a house on each corner

3. Explain to the group that without strong foundations (hygiene factors) you will not be able to move on to decorating the house. If there are no foundations, there is no point in investing in the house, which may not be there for long

4. To demonstrate, take one of the supports (shoe box) away and show how unstable the house is now. No amount of decorating and attention to the house will make it any more stable – you need to work on the foundations first

5. Ask them to make the link to the motivation theory

What's the point?

To emphasise the need for managers to be aware that, unless the hygiene factors are addressed, they will always struggle with motivating their staff.

PEOPLE MANAGEMENT

BALLOON BALANCING

Group size
Minimum 6 -
maximum 15

Time
20 minutes

Aim
Convince new managers to balance their priorities for great team results

Learning
Use John Adair's model of leadership to prioritise the responsibilities of your new role

List the positive effects of paying attention to each area of responsibility on John Adair's model

List the negative effects of paying little or no attention to each area of responsibility on John Adair's model

Materials
Nine balloons
Marker pen
String

Trainer knowledge needed
Familiarity with John Adair's model of leadership that emphasises
'team, task and individual'. Refer to John Adair's Action Centred Leadership model,
which is a common theme in most of his books. One example is *Effective
Leadership Skills*

Process
1. Introduce John Adair's management model
2. Inflate all the balloons to various sizes
3. Tie them together in twos and threes
4. Write on them: Task, Team and Individual
5. Split group into subgroups
6. Give one set of balloons to each group

Process cont'd

7. Ask them to discuss the possible impact of being part of a team where the manager focuses upon each of the three areas of responsibility in the percentages represented by the size of the balloons. For instance, if one set of balloons has a large 'team' balloon, a small 'individual' balloon and a non-existent 'task' balloon:

- What would the team be like?
- How would it feel?
- What behaviour would be rewarded?

- What would the benefits/drawbacks be?
- Who would like/dislike being part of the team?
- What sort of leader would this team have?

8. Discuss thinking as a large group

What's the point?

This is a very visual and hands-on way of demonstrating the three circles of the model without having to draw it on the flipchart.

Variation

Use in a teambuild. After you have explained the concept, give the team non-inflated balloons and ask them to inflate them, and join them together to represent the team as they see it.

EAT THAT FROG! (TIME MANAGEMENT)

Group size
Any

Time
30 minutes

Aim
Start your time management course with a bang

Learning
Discuss the causes of various forms of procrastination

Materials
Loaf of bread, paintbrushes, various food colourings (to be used as paints)
Hundreds and thousands, and other edible toppings

Trainer knowledge needed
Time management

Process

1. At the beginning of the day, perhaps as part of a group introduction or icebreaker, discover from the delegates what small insect or animal they have a fear or an abhorrence of. This will lead into your scene-setting activity to begin your time management course

2. Pair up delegates. Hand out two slices of bread per delegate

3. In their pairs ask delegates to remind each other what insect or animal they mentioned a loathing or fear of

4. With no more than two slices of bread, ask them each to artistically mould their bread into a sculpture of their partner's feared or loathed subject

5. Additionally they must bring the moulded bread to life by painting it as they see fit using the food colourings, etc provided. Once completed, they hand the sculpture back to their 'friend'

6. Explain to the group that one of the tasks they must complete between now and the end of the day is to eat their awful sculpture!!!

Process cont'd

7. Draw the links between the sculpture and the tasks that we put off, because they seem scary or involve something that we hate doing

8. Allow these sculptures to sit in front of them during the day – but remain alert and capitalise on opportunities to make (light-hearted) comments when you spot a delegate nibbling, and make connections between the way they approach this less than appealing task to the way they might approach non-desirable tasks at work

Possible delegate reactions and ways to draw the links:
- Stuffing it down: getting an awful job done first (eating that frog).
  Every other task during the day will seem pleasant by comparison!
- Slicing it up and eating a bit at a time during the day: breaking an ugly task down into step-by-step activities – then beginning with the first one and working your way through
- Staring at it, talking about it or doing something else instead: procrastinating
- Eating a little: job half done. No plan, deadline, motivation
- Not eating it at all: task undone. No motivation to do it

And to the question, 'What if I am faced with two sculptures to devour?' answer, 'Eat the ugliest one first'.

What's the point?
This is a fun exercise to provide some context and bring to life the realities of good time management. It works well when used in conjunction with the principles laid out in Brian Tracy's book *Eat that Frog*.

PEOPLE MANAGEMENT

RISKY BUSINESS (HEALTH & SAFETY)

Group size
Any

Time
30 minutes

Aim
To have fun while simplifying the purpose of a risk assessment

Learning
Identify potential hazards from a picture

Materials
Pictures of everyday scenes, containing potential hazards, either obvious or subtle (collect from magazines, newspapers, you and your friends)
Numbered A4 paper (as many numbers as you have pictures)
Prizes (sweets, toys, etc)

Trainer knowledge needed
Risk assessment basics

Process
1. Hang up the pictures around the room and number them

2. Split your group into pairs

3. Give each pair A4 paper with numbers 1 to however many pictures you have

4. In their pairs, ask them to wander around the room with their paper until they have looked at each picture. Based on what is going on in the picture, their task is to make a guess as to 'what happens next?' and write their prediction for each picture next to the relevant number

5. Tell them that prizes will be issued to the pair with the best prediction, eg: the most creative, the story that makes use of all the elements in the picture, the one told most convincingly

6. Ask each pair to nominate their best effort (no need to hear all the stories) to share with the group

7. While one pair reads out their pessimistic prediction, ask the others to issue 0-10 points as a ranking for how the prediction met each of the above criteria

8. Add up points for each and issue prize/s

9. Make connections between the exercise and the practical purpose of risk assessment

What's the point?

Risk assessment is based upon our ability to spot potential hazards.

PEOPLE MANAGEMENT

BEHAVIOURAL INTERVIEWING

Group size
Any, but preferably an even number

Time
20 minutes

Aim
To reinforce the theory behind competency interviewing by encouraging people to reflect upon moments of their life when they have achieved high performance

Learning
Practise the technique of behavioural interviewing

Materials
Prompt cards with questions (see page 94)

Trainer knowledge needed
Thorough understanding of the theory of competency interviewing and where it originated. For further reading see *The Interviewer's Pocketbook* by John Townsend

Process

1. Split the group into pairs

2. Explain that the purpose of the exercise is to understand why behavioural interviewing is so effective in recruiting people

3. Give out the cards that introduce the opening types of questions and then encourage the use of probing questions to draw out a time when they felt as if they were having a peak moment, or in Maslow's terms, self-actualised

Suggestions for questions on card:

1. Think about a time when you felt as if you were in the 'flow of things'
2. What happened?
3. What was the situation?
4. What did you do?
5. How did it feel?
6. What was in your mind?
7. What made you do what you did?
8. How did you know it was the right thing to do?
9. What did you learn from the situation?
10. What would you do differently if you had the situation again?

What's the point?
The point is to get them practising the core skills of behavioural interviewing or competency interviewing without attaching it to a set of competencies required for a particular job or role.

TEAM

MY TEAM AS I SEE IT

Group size
Maximum
15

Time
20 minutes

Aim
Provide an opportunity for teams to move forward

Learning
Identify and discuss team issues
Clarify your viewpoint
Hear the viewpoint of others

Materials
Large white paper
tablecloth
Lots of coloured pens

Trainer knowledge needed
Knowledge of facilitation skills to draw out and focus the conversation

Process
1. Ensure that room layout is boardroom style. That means one square with everyone sitting round the table
2. Allow 15 minutes for the team to decorate the table using the materials supplied, to represent how they see the team right **now**
3. You leave the room
4. Return after the time has expired and ask them to talk you through what they have done and why

What's the point?
With this exercise, there is not necessarily just one place that you will end up. The main purpose is to get the team discussing, drawing and working together from the outset.

Variation
Ask them to decorate the tablecloth, as they would **like** the team to be in the future after the teambuild.

BELBIN TEAM ROLES

Group size
Minimum
9

Time
20 minutes

Aim
Bring to life and make memorable the Belbin team roles

Learning
Identify the different team roles from a series of clues
Identify the stereotypical Belbin team roles from the props others have used for dressing up

Materials
Nine cards (you will need to write all the team roles on the cards, one on each.) String (enough for nine 'card medallions'). Attach the string to both ends of the card so that you now have a very large name card medallion.

Suggested props:
- Shaper – Maggie Thatcher mask or Hitler moustache and whip (control)
- Co-ordinator – Film Director's 'action' board (bringing it all together)
- Plant – A wacky coloured hat or braces (something a bit different)

- Teamworker – Teddy bear/large gloves (caring/touchy-feely)
- Monitor Evaluator – Can of non-alcoholic lager plus judge's wig (sober-minded and judges things well)
- Completer Finisher – Giant magnifying glass (details)
- Resource Investigator – Large inflatable mobile phone (making contacts)
- Implementer – Large glasses plus a serious expression (practical; gets the job done)
- Specialist – Technical journal or newspaper (constantly learning in a focused way)

Trainer knowledge needed

A thorough understanding of the nine Belbin team roles is essential

Process

1. Give a ten-minute overview of what the Belbin team roles are about

2. Ask for nine volunteers and ask them to come up, one by one

3. As each person approaches you, give them one of the props associated with the team type and say nothing to them except, 'thanks, now please sit down again'.

4. Once all props have been given out, ask group to identify who is portraying each role

5. As they get it right, ask them questions such as, 'what gave it away for you?' and 'what were the clues that helped you?'

6. As each role is identified, give out the pre-prepared 'card medallion' for them to wear

What's the point?

This will give your delegates a break from the theory of team roles. Plus, it is a light-hearted way of getting people to remember the roles. You can guarantee that the people who volunteered will never forget the role they were.

Variation

1. As a review activity, ask them to mime a role they have learnt, for rest of group to guess

2. The trainer should put on each separate prop as they explain the different roles. This, coupled with some mild dramatics, will make for easier recall

TEAM

MEET THE TEAM

Group size
Minimum 8 - maximum 40

Time
30 minutes

Aim
For people to get to know each other

Learning
Delegates will be able to identify each other's personalised t-shirt

Materials
A cheap, plain white t-shirt for each delegate
Lots of marker/colouring pens

Trainer knowledge needed
None

Process

1. Give every delegate a t-shirt each and invite them to get themselves lots of pens

2. Ask them to spend 15 minutes decorating the t-shirt to personalise it. Suggest they decorate it with things that show previous jobs, hobbies, interests, why they like their current job so much, pictures of what they would rather be doing if they were not there (!) and any other personal information they are willing to share

3. When they have finished, hang the t-shirts up around the room with flipchart paper beneath them

4. Ask people to wander around and guess who the t-shirt was made by. They need to write down the person's name under the t-shirt and say why

5. Once everyone has written something underneath each t-shirt, ask the owners to own up

6. Take the group through a review of what they have written and why

What's the point?
This is designed to get people to know each other. It works particularly
well with the larger group (15+) as people's knowledge of individuals is not so great.

Variation
1. Instead of hanging the t-shirts up on the wall, throw them into the middle of the room
   for people to get more 'hands on'

2. Instead of the flipchart paper underneath each t-shirt on the wall, give people
   clipboards to go around with and write their answers on. At the end, ask them to
   read out what they have, and award prizes for the person with the most correct
   answers

3. Similar to 2. above, give people a time limit and play loud energetic music to get them
   running around

NOTES

TRAINER TRAINING

THE BRAIN

Group size
Any

Time
30 minutes

Aim
To consciously use either left or right brain hemispheres
to achieve a desired outcome

Learning
List the favoured job of each
side of the brain
Demonstrate the activity of a brain
when solving a problem

Materials
Hat with the words 'The Discriminative
Faculty' on it
Optional – other hats with 'Mental
Monkey' on them
Flipchart paper and pens

Trainer knowledge needed
How the brain works

Process

1. Give an overview of the various parts of the brain and how research can now demonstrate how the left and right sides of the brain have developed a preference for working on particular problems

2. List the preferences of each

3. Tell them that our objective, armed with this knowledge, is to enlist the help of **both** sides of the brain to solve problems, so that we can achieve more effective results

4. Ask the group to partake in an activity to practise using the brain more deliberately

5. Pick someone in the group whom you know to be more knowledgeable in a particular field than the other members of the group. (If they are more senior too, that might help.) Ask them to put on 'The Discriminative Faculty' hat and come up to the front and stand by the flipchart

6. Ask the rest of the group to wear the 'Mental Monkey' hats

7. Inform them all that the ability to discriminate is very much a left brain activity – very useful for choosing the right course of action. Mental monkey-like chatter that goes on in our heads is a right brain activity – useful for coming up with ideas. They are now acting as representatives of these parts of the brain

A. TRAINER

Process cont'd

8. Ask the volunteer at the front to identify an unsolved issue they are faced with at the moment and state this to the group

9. The group's job is to blurt out as many ideas related to this issue as they can think of which may help. There are no rules, and no judgement will be passed upon them

10. The volunteer's job is to collect the ideas on the flipchart exactly as they are said. They must suspend judgement, must offer no advice, extra information or feedback. In other words, they must put the discriminative part of themselves on hold

11. Let the activity run

12. Ask the volunteer how they felt during the activity. How about the mental monkeys?

What's the point?
It can be very hard to stop applying knowledge or logic to the way we approach solving a problem, and instead allow our creative brain to help us. This exercise helps to demonstrate that fact.

TRAINER TRAINING

FACILITATION SKILLS

**Group
size**
Any

Time
15 minutes

Aim
Introduce the core skills of a facilitator in a novel way

Learning
Identify some of the core skills of a facilitator
Discuss the basics of facilitation including listening
skills, observation, awareness of team
dynamics, neutrality/non-judgement

Materials
One judge's wig
Swiss cheese
Cut out paper question marks
Set of plastic ears
Large pair of glasses
Pair of rubber hands

Trainer knowledge needed
Thorough understanding of facilitation skills

PARDON

Process

1. Lay out all the props on a table at the front of the room. Ideally they should be clearly visible when the delegates arrive
2. After the normal introductions, ask the group to pick up any of the objects that they want to
3. Ask them to spend a few minutes thinking about how the objects could relate to facilitation skills
4. Review the answers as one big group and record on flipchart

What's the point?

All of the objects relate symbolically to some of the core skills of facilitating. There are no wrong answers to this; however, the following are pointers to look for:

- Judge's wig – either non-judgemental or judging what the best course of action should be when facilitating
- Swiss cheese – this is linked to neutrality in the role of facilitator. Switzerland is known for its neutrality
- Set of ears – listening skills
- Question marks – questioning skills
- Large pair of glasses – observation skills
- Rubber gloves – 'touchy-feely'. The ability to pick up on the subtleties that are occurring during a facilitated event

TRAINER TRAINING

NEVER A 'X' WORD

A. TRAINER

Group
size
Minimum 4

Time
15 minutes

Aim
Create an experience where your delegates will be forced to use different parts of the brain

Learning
Identify the key differences between left- and right-brain activities
Relate how activities completed are linked to our use of different parts of the brain

Materials
Large piece of paper
Blu-Tack

Trainer knowledge needed
Knowledge of accelerated learning, particularly the triune brain concept.
For more information, please refer to www.kaizen-training.com

A. TRAINER

Process

1. Copy the crossword on the next page onto a large piece of paper or four pieces of flipchart put together

2. Split group into small groups of four people

3. Allow ten minutes to solve the puzzle. If you have more than one group, consider setting it up as a competition

4. Allow five minutes to review the answers

What's the point?

While solving the puzzle, delegates will use a wide variety of methods including logic, guessing, movement, fun, etc. They may then use their experiences to draw the links to the part of their brain they were favouring, and the alternative options open to them.

Variation

1. Copy the crossword onto separate sheets of A4 and use as a placemat for each delegate's seat space. They can fill it out during that awkward silence at the beginning of a course

2. Draw a huge brain behind the crossword itself to make it more visual

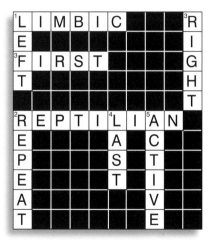

A. TRAINER

Across
1 Emotional part of brain (6)
2 Primitive part of brain (9)
3 Memory most powerful now (5)

Down
1 Side of brain (4)
2 Memory technique (6)
3 One side of brain (5)
4 Powerful memory point (4)
5 Movement helps memory (6)

Note: You can add more if you need to

TRAINER TRAINING

APPLYING PRESENTATION SKILLS

Group size
6 - 10

Time
30 minutes at beginning of course,
30 minutes at end

Aim
Contrast the level of skill and confidence of your group at the start of a presentation skills course with the level attained by the end

Learning
Build confidence when talking in public
Develop skills for presenting in public
Have fun

Materials

Two containers (hats 1 and 2)

Coloured cards with the following words written on: 'Beginning, Body, Conclusion'; 'The 3 Tellums'; '3 - 5 second unbroken eye contact'; 'Bang'; 'Pause for effect'

Different coloured cards with the names of various well-known sports, places, hobbies and news story headlines

Trainer knowledge needed

Knowledge of the tools and skills required for effective presenting. You may wish to adjust the names of the techniques above to be in line with the names of the skills in your own course

Process (part 1)

1. Introduce the subject of presenting

2. Ask the delegates to write as many discussion topics as they can on scraps of paper. Place these in hat 1

Note: If no/few subjects are forthcoming use/supplement with your own pre-prepared list above

A. TRAINER

3. Call for volunteers to stand at the front of the room and talk for two minutes about the subject that they must pull at random from hat 1

4. After the presentation, give the presenter one minute to say how they were feeling during it. Summarise their answers on the top part of a flipchart with their name at the top

5. Allow your group 20-30 seconds each to feedback to the presenter a positive fact about their presentation style. Add these facts to the bottom of the person's flipchart

6. Stick all participants' flipchart sheets on the wall

7. Now deliver your presentation skills course

Process (part 2)
At the end of the course:

1. Refer the delegates back to the exercise at the start of your course

2. Ask them to participate one more time for another two minutes using the same subjects already in hat 1

3. However, this time they must pick one subject from hat 1 (the subject on which they must talk) and a second subject from hat 2. This will be a presentation technique, which has been discussed during your course

4. Delegates must present their subject to the group and make a conscious effort to demonstrate the skill named on their card while doing so

5. As before, they will summarise how it went for them. Did using the technique help or hinder? Why? How were they feeling?

6. The rest of the group, as part of their feedback, will guess at the skill they believe was on the presenter's card

7. Refer to their self and group feedback flipcharts from part 1. Discuss as a group what has changed between the first and second presentations they delivered

What's the point?
This gets delegates presenting in a fun and threat-free environment and provides an opportunity to compare their pre-presentation course performance with a post-course one.

AIM - FIRE!

Group size
Any

Time
20 - 30 minutes

Aim
Write clear presentation aims

Learning
Debate what a clear aim should be saying
Consistently identify what a true aim looks like

Materials
Coloured sticky dots
6 double-sided targets (print off from clip-art or make with card)
Print and cut out each 'aim' below:

A. To talk to the team about timekeeping
B. To convince my colleagues to recycle waste paper

A. TRAINER

C. To persuade the marketing department to seek advice from us regarding the new brochure
D. To persuade managers to give feedback to their staff
E. To run through the restructuring of the department
F. To get people to make a donation to the local animal charity
G. To teach the front of house staff how to use the new computer system
H. To put staff in the right mood to enjoy the office Christmas party
I. To discuss the next sales promotion
J. To persuade the Managing Director to provide finances for a new workshop
K. To run through work in progress
L. To encourage colleagues to make personal calls only at off-peak times

Trainer knowledge needed

Difference between effective and ineffective aims. For more information please refer to *The Business Presenter's Pocketbook* by John Townsend

Process

1. Print off and cut out each individual aim – or make your own
2. Make six double-sided targets
3. Stick aims A - F in the middle of one side of each target
4. Stick aims G - L in the middle of the other side of each target

A. TRAINER

Process cont'd

5. Split group into pairs
6. Hand out 12 coloured sticky dots to each pair, ensuring that they have a unique colour to identify themselves by
7. Put out the targets so that aims A - F are on view
8. Ask the pairs to study each aim and stick one sticky dot on each one they agree to be a 'true' aim. They should place the dot near or far from the centre of the target, to illustrate visually how well they think the aim hits the mark
9. Check the answers, discuss as a large group and discover if there were any disagreements between people in each pair.
   Note: A and E are not true aims but rather something you might do while working toward an aim
10. When you are satisfied that everyone is clear as to why A and E are not aims and the others are, turn the targets around and ask them to complete the same activity again, using their remaining dots
11. Again check answers and discuss as a large group

What's the point?

Learning to write clear aims that 'hit the target' is a fundamental starting point for anyone wishing to begin writing a presentation.

About the Authors

Paul Tizzard is a Director of Inspirit Training Ltd. He also has an eclectic work background from coach cleaner to Virgin Atlantic's Management Development Consultant. Paul set up Inspirit Training Ltd in October 2001 and specialises in management development, individual effectiveness and trainer development. He also derives a great deal of pleasure from facilitating and coaching – both doing and training it.

Paul's style of delivery is very practical and relaxed. He needs to know that the material is getting through to the audience.

Paul can be contacted at paul@in-spirit.co.uk and +44 1737 844566

Alan Evans is a Learning and Development consultant. He has worked in more jobs than you can wave a stick at. His broad range of experience gives him the unique ability to relate to anyone and to have some understanding of 'where they are coming from'. Alan has a very punchy style of delivery that creates fantastic impact during any learning event.

Alan can be contacted at alan@madetomeasuretraining.co.uk

Cartoon by Alan Evans (shows Paul & Alan)

ORDER FORM

Your details	*Please send me:*

Your details

Name _____

Position _____

Company _____

Address _____

_____

_____

Telephone _____

Fax _____

E-mail _____

VAT No. (EC companies) _____

Your Order Ref _____

Please send me:

No. copies

The Icebreakers _____ Pocketbook ☐

The _____ Pocketbook ☐

The _____ Pocketbook ☐

The _____ Pocketbook ☐

The _____ Pocketbook ☐

Order by Post
MANAGEMENT POCKETBOOKS LTD
LAUREL HOUSE, STATION APPROACH, ALRESFORD,
HAMPSHIRE SO24 9JH UK

Order by Phone, Fax or Internet
Telephone: +44 (0)1962 735573
Facsimile: +44 (0)1962 733637
E-mail: sales@pocketbook.co.uk
Web: www.pocketbook.co.uk

Customers in USA should contact:
Stylus Publishing, LLC, 22883 Quicksilver Drive,
Sterling, VA 20166-2012
Telephone: 703 661 1581 or 800 232 0223
Facsimile: 703 661 1501 E-mail: styluspub@aol.com